American Hero Day

by Alice Cary
Illustrated by Barbara Kiwak

Editorial Offices: Glenview, Illinois • Parsippany, New Jersey • New York, New York
Sales Offices: Needham, Massachusetts • Duluth, Georgia • Glenview, Illinois
Coppell, Texas • Sacramento, California • Mesa, Arizona

The second graders were ready for American Hero Day. Tonight their parents would come to see the children's work. Each child had painted a mask of a famous American.

But many of the masks were a mess. A cat had run inside the school. The cat stepped in paint and ran on the masks.

"Oh no! The masks are ruined!" said Mr. Brown, the teacher.

"What can we do?" Carlos asked. "Who will save our day? We need our own hero."

"We can paint new masks," Mary said.

"There isn't time," Mr. Brown said.

"I have an idea," Carlos said. "Do you remember our visit to Baker School? They had Hero Day too. Maybe we can borrow their masks."

"That's a great idea!" Mr. Brown said. "I'll call Mrs. Clay, the teacher there."

Mr. Brown went to the office. He called Mrs. Clay.

"Yes, you may borrow our masks," Mrs. Clay said. She soon came with many masks.

"Mrs. Clay is our hero!" Mary said. Everyone felt better.

Soon parents filled the room.
They loved the art on the walls.
Everyone was excited.

The second graders came on stage.
Some had their own masks. Some had
masks from Baker School. The masks
were art, too.

"There are many great Americans,"
Mary said. "There are many great
heroes."

"Today we had a problem," Mr.
Brown said. "A cat almost ruined
our day."

"But Carlos had a super idea," Mr.
Brown said. "Carlos was our own hero."

Each student showed a mask.

"My mask is Ben Franklin," Carlos said. "He helped the USA to be free."

"My mask is Sally Ride," Mary said. "She flew in space."

Everyone clapped for the American heroes. Everyone clapped for the second-grade class.